WORKING HARD WITH TONKA TRUCKS

Contents

WORKING HARD WITH THE BUSY FIRE TRUCK
Written by Jordan Horowitz

WORKING HARD WITH THE MIGHTY DUMP TRUCK
Written by Justine Korman

WORKING HARD WITH THE MIGHTY MIXER
Written by Francine Hughes

WORKING HARD WITH THE MIGHTY LOADER
Written by Justine Korman

Illustrated by Steven James Petruccio

ISBN 0-439-44528-0

TONKA is a trademark of Hasbro.
Used with permission.
© 2002 Hasbro.
All Rights Reserved. Published by Scholastic Inc.
SCHOLASTIC and associated logos are trademarks and/or registered trademarks of Scholastic Inc.

10 9 8 7 6 5 4 3 2 1   02 03 04 05 06

Printed in the U.S.A.
First Scholastic printing, October 2002

SCHOLASTIC INC.
New York   Toronto   London   Auckland   Sydney
Mexico City   New Delhi   Hong Kong   Buenos Aires

Tonka®

WORKING HARD WITH THE BUSY FIRE TRUCK™

Written by Jordan Horowitz
Illustrated by Steven James Petruccio

SCHOLASTIC INC.

New York   Toronto   London   Auckland   Sydney

Fire fighter Tom arrives at the fire station bright and early.
"Good morning!" he calls to the other fire fighters.

Every day the fire fighters take turns doing different jobs. Today it's Tom's turn to check the fire truck. First he inspects the fire hoses.

He turns on the headlights, and he makes sure the siren is working.

Then he washes the truck
and fills the gas tank
with fuel. Now the fire truck
is ready for action!

The other fire fighters clean the fire station.
One polishes the fire pole.
Another tidies up the kitchen.
All the fire fighters work hard to keep
their fire station neat and clean.

The fire chief gathers all the fire fighters together.
He gives each one a special fire truck assignment.
Bob will be in charge of the water pumper controls.

Sam will drive
the truck.

And Tom will handle the nozzle at the top of the ladder.
Now the fire fighters are ready for any fire emergency.

Soon the warning chimes sound over the loudspeaker.
BING-BONG! BING-BONG! "Emergency! Emergency!"
calls the dispatcher. "Highway 17, north of town!"

The fire fighters charge into action.
They put on their boots and fireproof coats.
Then they grab their helmets and run to the fire truck.

Tom slides open the huge fire station door.
He directs the fire truck out to the street.

WHEE-OOH! WHEE-OOH! WHEE-OOH!
The speedy fire truck heads to the rescue!

The fire truck drives up to a farm.
There's smoke coming from the barn!
But the fire fighters are in time to
stop the fire before it spreads.

Then Tom sees a tiny kitten trapped on the barn roof!

He knows just what to do.
Up, up, up goes the long ladder.
Then up climbs Tom to rescue the helpless kitten.

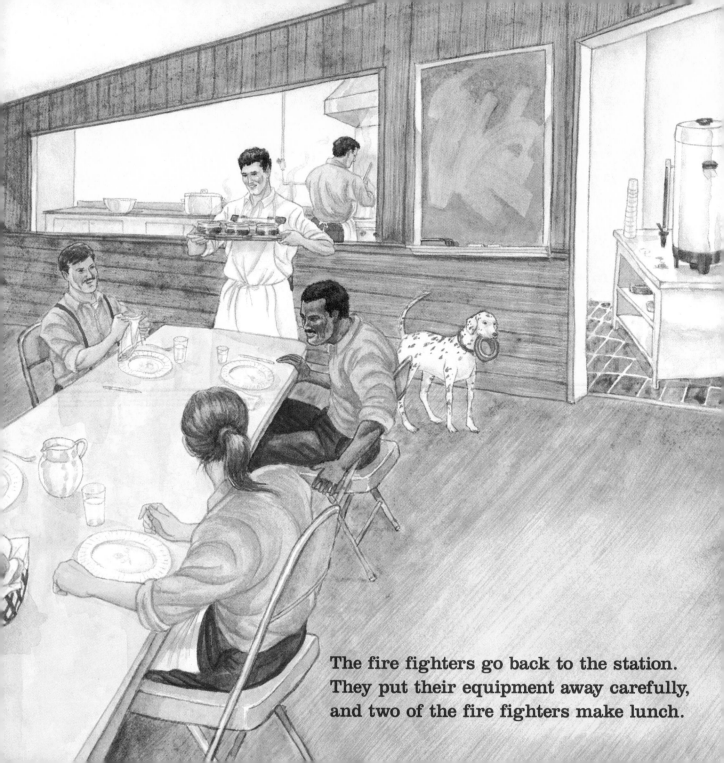

The fire fighters go back to the station.
They put their equipment away carefully,
and two of the fire fighters make lunch.

But before everyone can sit down,
the chimes sound again.
BING-BONG! BING-BONG!
"Emergency!" cries the dispatcher.
"There's a fire at Fourth and Elm!"
All the fire fighters rush from the table.

And within seconds the fire truck
is speeding through the city streets.
WHEE-OOH! WHEE-OOH!

Cars and trucks pull over to let the fire truck go by.
People stay out of the way, too.

There's the fire!
A police car and an ambulance are already on the scene.

Sam parks the fire truck carefully, trying not to take up too
much space in front of the burning department store.
Other emergency vehicles are on the way!

Here comes a pumper truck.
It is filled with extra water.

Here is an aerial ladder truck.
It helps rescue people from high windows.

The fire chief jumps out of his pickup
truck. He gives his crew a plan
for fighting the fire.

Some of the fire fighters put on their masks and air tanks.
They race into the building. A few carry fire extinguishers.
Others carry axes and crowbars to help them get past locked doors.

Tom and Bob will fight the fire from outside the building.
Tom raises the fire ladder until it reaches the top floor.

Bob attaches a special tube to a fire hydrant.
Now the water can flow easily to the nozzle
at the top of the ladder.

Then up climbs Tom.
He aims the nozzle
at the flames.
WHOOSH! The water
puts out the fire!

The fire chief checks the building inside and out.
When he is sure there is no more danger,
he sends his team back to the station.

Back at the firehouse the fire fighters hang up their gear.
They are very tired, and they're hungrier than ever.
But Tom isn't ready to sit down for lunch.

Today it's Tom's job to keep the fire truck clean.
So he washes all the grimy dirt away.
Soon the fire truck is shiny and spotless.
And ready for the next fire emergency!

Tonka®

WORKING HARD WITH
THE MIGHTY DUMP TRUCK™

Written by Justine Korman
Illustrated by Steven James Petruccio

SCHOLASTIC
New York Toronto London Auckland Sydney

Dan the Mighty Dump Truck driver gets an early start.
He and his dump truck have a busy day ahead.
First Dan makes sure the truck has a full tank of fuel.

Then Dan and the Mighty Dump Truck are on their way.
At this hour, other busy trucks are on the road, too.

Soon Dan arrives at the construction site.
Other trucks are already hard at work on a brand-new road.
Each one has a special job to do.

The bulldozer cuts the ground where it is too high
and fills it in where it is too low.
The backhoe digs up a small hill.

The loader piles dirt into the bed at the back of Dan's truck.
Load after load goes into the big bed.
The Mighty Dump Truck can hold a lot of dirt!

Dan drives to the other side of the construction site.
Dirt is needed there to fill in a ditch.
The Mighty Dump Truck's engine roars as it moves
the heavy load of dirt.

Dan works the controls in the dump truck's cab.
The front end of the truck bed lifts, and dirt pours out
the back. After many loads of dirt, the ditch is finally filled in.

Graders and bulldozers make the new road level, while Dan gets ready for the next job. A loader fills the Mighty Dump Truck's bed with stones.

Dan drives slowly along the new dirt road.
He lifts the Mighty Dump Truck's bed to pour out a
layer of stones. As the bed empties, the front end
lifts higher and higher.

A layer of sand will go on top of the stones.
A giant hopper pours sand into the big bed of Dan's
Mighty Dump Truck.

Dan carefully works the controls in the truck's cab to dump the sand on top of the stones.
Behind the truck a grader moves slowly along, leveling out the sand.

Now the new road is ready to be paved with asphalt.
And the truck drivers are ready for lunch.
Dan spots one of his favorite trucks — a hot dog truck!

After lunch, Dan's Mighty Dump Truck takes a load of dirt to another construction site. Suddenly Dan hears a siren wail.

He pulls over to the right side of the road to let two
fire trucks pass. One is the pumper truck.
The other carries the rescue ladders.

The fire chief's truck goes speeding by after the fire engines.
Dan doesn't mind pulling over for emergency vehicles.
Those trucks have an important job to do.

The Mighty Dump Truck is doing an important job, too.
The dirt it carries will help make the foundation for
a new apartment building where families will live.

Many trucks work together to put up a big building. Dan's Mighty Dump Truck pours its load of dirt onto the foundation while cranes, bulldozers, and excavators lift, carry, and dig.

Dump trucks, big and small, bring in more and more dirt.
A sturdy building must have a firm foundation.

Soon it's time to mix concrete. Dan's Mighty Dump Truck dumps a load of sand into a huge cement mixer. The mixer spins the sand with gravel, cement, and water to make concrete.

When the concrete is ready, it is poured into the foundation. The concrete will dry overnight.

At the end of the day, Dan drives home in his
Mighty Dump Truck. On the highway he passes big
delivery trucks and moving vans. Some of these trucks
will drive all night long.

But Dan and his Mighty Dump Truck need some rest.
Tomorrow will be another busy day!

Tonka®
WORKING HARD WITH THE MIGHTY MIXER™

Written by Francine Hughes
Illustrated by Steven James Petruccio

SCHOLASTIC INC.
New York   Toronto   London   Auckland   Sydney

Mike drives a Mighty Mixer. His job is to bring
concrete to construction sites. Each morning
Mike goes to the plant where concrete is made.

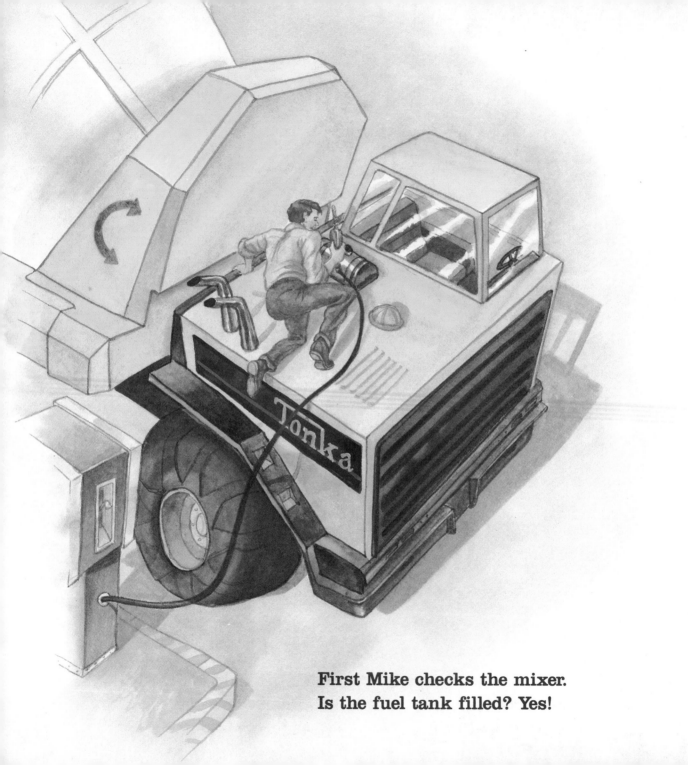

First Mike checks the mixer.
Is the fuel tank filled? Yes!

Do the tires need air? No! The Mighty Mixer
is ready to go.

Mike drives the Mighty Mixer under a tower called a batch plant. Cement, sand, gravel, and water are all mixed together inside. Out pours the wet, heavy concrete — right into the mixer's drum!

But the concrete isn't ready yet! It needs
more mixing. Mike pulls a lever inside the
mixer's cab. *Whir. Whir.* The drum starts
to turn.

It keeps turning and mixing, mixing and turning as Mike drives to the construction site — an elementary school.

Rat-a-tat-tat! Rat-a-tat-tat! Jackhammers
are breaking up parts of the old school
yard. A loader carries away the rubble.

Then the workers build a form. They place strips
of wood around the school yard. This form will
hold the concrete in place until it hardens.
Once the form is ready, Mike's job begins.

Mike lowers the chute at the back of the
Mighty Mixer. Then he pulls another lever
inside the cab. *Whir. Whir.* Now the drum
is turning the other way.

Concrete pours out of the truck, down the chute, and into place.

A worker smooths out the concrete.

When it dries,
the wooden form will
be removed.

Then schoolchildren will be able to play
in the brand-new school yard.

Later in the week, Mike is on his way
to help build an apartment building.
First, backhoes and dump trucks get
the site ready.

They dig, dig, dig the dirt. Then they haul it away. Again and again the trucks do their jobs until the hole in the ground is wide and even.

Now it's time for the foundation. Everything else will be built on top of that. Mike starts by pouring some concrete into a wheelbarrow. He realizes the mixture needs water. It's easy to add — the Mighty Mixer has its very own water tank.

Once again the drum spins round and round.
This time the concrete is just right.
It comes pouring out of the mixer. Soon it
fills the hole. The foundation is made.
Mike's job is finished.

Back at the plant, Mike washes down the Mighty Mixer. Then he pours water into the drum, and the truck churns the water out — just like it's concrete.

Now the Mighty Mixer is clean inside
and out, and ready for work tomorrow.

Mike's next job is to help build a highway.
He drives along a bumpy dirt road to begin work.
Big dump trucks and other machines are already
there, doing their part to clear the way.

Once the dirt road is ready, Mike's job begins.
The concrete is poured as the Mighty Mixer moves
along. Right behind the mixer is a spreading
machine, working to smooth out the bumps.

After the concrete has dried and the road
has been paved, people will have a new
highway — and a faster way to get to the city.

Today Mike's job is to help build
a new airline terminal in the middle of
a busy airport.

There are lots of other mixers at the site. Each truck pours its load into a different part of the foundation to make the job go more quickly.

Bit by bit, the building grows taller and taller. The Mighty Mixer helps make heavy slabs of concrete.

Then the cranes lift these heavy slabs up to the top floor of the building. This airline terminal is made mostly of steel and concrete.

Mike likes working with the Mighty Mixer.
He is always busy. His next job might
be to help make concrete blocks for a tunnel . . .

. . . or to help pour the concrete beams
for a bridge.

Mike and the Mighty Mixer might pour
the foundation for a movie theater . . .

. . . or add a new ramp to a skateboard park!

Mike enjoys doing many different jobs.
That's why he likes driving the
Mighty Mixer!

Tonka®

WORKING HARD WITH THE MIGHTY LOADER™

Written by Justine Korman
Illustrated by Steven James Petruccio

SCHOLASTIC INC.

New York   Toronto   London   Auckland   Sydney

Steve drives a Mighty Loader.
He is always busy. This week
he has six different jobs.

MONDAY. Steve and his loader are on their way to help build a new store. This job is miles away in the city.

But the Mighty Loader is too slow to ride on the highway.
So a powerful dump truck carries the loader on a trailer.
Steve rides in front with the dump truck driver.

Soon Steve and his loader arrive at the construction site.

Even though it's early morning, the construction site is already busy.

"Thanks for the lift!" Steve tells the dump truck driver.

Then he carefully backs his loader down from the trailer.

A bulldozer and a backhoe are hard at work preparing the foundation for the new store. Steve's job is to remove the loose dirt piled up around the hole.

He scoops up a heap of dirt with the loader's big bucket.
Steve uses the controls inside the cab to move the
bucket. He knows just how much dirt to pick up.
Taking too little would slow down the work. If he
takes too much, the dirt could spill out the back.

Steve lifts the loader's bucket over the side of a
big dump truck. He tilts the bucket to empty the
dirt into the dump truck's bed. The dirt thumps and
the rocks clang as they hit the empty, metal truck bed.

But the dump truck doesn't stay empty long! All through the day, Steve and the Mighty Loader fill up one dump truck after another. Steve and the loader work hard!

TUESDAY. Steve and the Mighty Loader are helping
to make a new road to a school. A grader breaks up
the hard dirt with its metal blade.

A bulldozer levels the ground and pushes the dirt to the side of the road. Back and forth all day, Steve's loader carries the dirt away.

On the way home, the loader moves slowly.
It is a heavy piece of equipment, so it can't go fast.
Steve lets the other drivers pass him on the road.

But nobody is allowed to pass a school bus.
Steve waits behind the bus until everyone gets
off and the red lights stop flashing.

WEDNESDAY. Today Steve is at the zoo. But he isn't going to visit the animals.

Steve and the Mighty Loader are helping to make ditches for pipes. They remove the dirt that the large trencher digs out.

When the ditches are ready, a crane lowers the pipes into place.

These pipes will bring fresh water to the new Penguin Palace.

When his job is done, Steve watches the cement mixer pour concrete. The mixer whirs round and round. Then a chute is lowered and the concrete comes pouring down.

It's the end of the day, and Steve stops at the snack truck for dinner. A special stove in the back of the truck is used to cook hamburgers and hot dogs. A small refrigerator keeps sodas and juice cans cold.

THURSDAY. Steve and the Mighty Loader are working on a farm. The farmer is leveling a new field for planting.

Fields have to be flat. Otherwise, low parts would get too much water and high parts would not get enough.

The farmer sells the soil he doesn't use to a
nursery, a store that grows and sells plants.
The nursery has sent a dump truck to
pick up the soil.

Steve wants to fill up the truck's bed evenly.
So he empties the loader's bucket into the front of
the dump truck's bed ... then the back ...
then the front again.

FRIDAY. Steve and the Mighty Loader have a very
different job today.

They are working at a coal mine.
Other loaders are already hard at work.

A special loader carries coal inside the narrow mine.
A crawler loader uses its heavy treads to roll over
soft sand.

Steve's loader fills a quarry dump truck with rocks.
Miners must dig through lots of rock before
they reach coal. The dump truck carries these rocks
away to be ground into gravel for roads.

SATURDAY. Steve and the Mighty Loader go to their last job. Today Steve is helping to build a new swimming pool in his neighborhood park.